Unlock your potential

*Chantelle,
Excited about working with you. Let's go to the next level. BE. DO. HAVE MORE.
xoxo Kimberly*

A Guided Journey for women ready to
BE MORE. DO MORE. HAVE MORE.

Kimberly S. Buchanan

#1 BEST SELLING AUTHOR

Copyright ©2017 by The Buchanan Group, LLC.

All rights reserved. No part of this publication may be reproduced, distributed, or transmitted in any form or by any means, including photocopying, recording, or other electronic or mechanical methods, without the prior written permission of the publisher, except in the case of brief quotations embodied in critical reviews and certain other noncommercial uses permitted by copyright law.

For permission requests, write to the author, addressed "Attention Permissions Coordinator," using the contact information below:

KimberlyBuchanan.com
@kimsbuchanan: Twitter, LinkedIn, and Instagram
@kimsbuchanan1: Facebook
#unlockyourpotentialbook

Content editor: Cindy Childress
Cover and interior design: Fran Johnson

ALL INQUIRIES: please email info@kimberlybuchanan.com
MEDIA + SPEAKING: please contact info@kimberlybuchanan.com

ISBN-13: 978-1979273961
ISBN-10: 1979273960

For David, Myles and Mason.
You are – and you always will be – the wind beneath my wings.

CONTENTS

Foreword 6

Introduction 8

REFLECTING ON THE PAST
Chapter 1:   Not Being Honest About Past Mistakes 11
Chapter 2:   Not Using What You Have 17
Chapter 3:   Thinking Small 23

NOT LETTING OTHERS CONTROL YOU
Chapter 4:   Guilt 29
Chapter 5:   Saying Yes To Everything 35
Chapter 6:   Wearing Your Heart On Your Sleeve 41

FINDING A GOOD SUPPORT SYSTEM
Chapter 7:   Pleasing Others 47
Chapter 8:   Not Asking For Help 53
Chapter 9:   Drags And Weights 59

TRUSTING YOURSELF AND YOUR MISSION
Chapter 10:   Being Scared To Put Yourself Out There 65
Chapter 11:   Talking Instead of Listening 71
Chapter 12:   Impatience 77

MAKING PRACTICAL CHANGES THAT PAY OFF LATER
Chapter 13:   Distractions 83
Chapter 14:   Social Media 89
Chapter 15:   Unhealthy Habits 95

SETTING REALISTIC EXPECTATIONS FOR YOURSELF AND OTHERS
Chapter 16:   Control 101
Chapter 17:   Perfectionism 107
Chapter 18:   Trying To Do It All 113

UNLOCKING NEW POTENTIAL AS YOU MOVE FORWARD
Chapter 19:   A Need To Lead and Not Follow 119
Chapter 20:   Competing 125
Chapter 21:   Excuses 131

FOREWORD
By CeCe President

> *Progress lies not in enhancing what is, but in advancing toward what will be.*
> *– Khalil Gibran*

YOU CAN BE, DO AND HAVE MORE. Imagine what life would look like if you accepted that these words were true for you. What lifelong dreams would you fulfill? What big, scary, audacious goal would you achieve? How fit, energetic, and healthy would you be? Imagine, if you believed these words were true for you, how different our children's lives might look.

If you're reading this book, I know that you're a woman who is committed to using her divine gifts, talents and abilities to create an amazing life for herself, her family and our world. Your 'MORE' isn't just fancy heels, designer dresses and a fabulous handbag (although we'd certainly have some of that as well), your 'MORE' is about creating and experiencing a world that has more joy, more abundance, more happiness and more love for all of our citizens. You're a woman who wants to make a difference while living your legacy. You're the kind of woman who serves on community boards, donates to hurricane relief in Houston and screams at the top of your lungs at your child's track meet.

You are a change agent. You are an armor bearer. You are a proponent of all that is good, right and beautiful.

Which is why we need you, more than anyone, to know that You can **Be, Do** and **Have More.** These simple words are a statement of fact. You can **Be, Do** and **Have More** of whatever it is that enlivens your soul, brings you joy, sets your heart aflame or fulfills your purpose.

Intellectually, I think most of us understand this about ourselves. Most people called to read a book titled *"Unlock Your Potential: A guided journey for women ready to be more, do more, have more"* would likely say of themselves, "yes, I do have potential. I can **Be, Do,** and **Have More.**" However, my intention is for you to not just "know it" at an intellectual level, my intention is for you to "own it" at a cellular level. Where at the core of your being, you live this truth and your potential becomes your present, regardless of any adversities, challenges or setbacks that may come your way during the process.

I must say, when it comes to adversities, challenges and setbacks, let me tell you, I am uniquely qualified to share. Long before I was a leadership expert, international speaker and coach, helping thousands of women across the globe create physical, financial and emotional freedom in their lives; I was a woman who found herself 50 pounds overweight, $2 million in debt and severely depressed after the loss of a once lucrative real estate investment firm. For a very long time, nearly two years to be exact, I absolutely laid down on my life. I didn't communicate with long-time friends or spend time with my family, I became reclusive, inactive and unmotivated. I had no faith, no confidence and no belief in myself to have anything. Yet, that unwavering truth that I COULD **Be, Do** and **Have** anything WAS still there.

I started by first just convincing myself that I could do 'a little'. A little just looked like actually getting out of the bed, showering (at least a few times a week anyway) and perhaps even listening to an inspirational message without turning it off. Then I started to believe that I could be 'ok'. When I was 'being ok', I found myself praying and meditating regularly, I participated in family walks in my neighborhood, journaled and talked about my experiences. When I started to remember that I have more, everything became different. I was up early, exercised daily, lived in gratitude and took massive action towards my goals. The result of unlocking my potential was another 7-figure business; partnerships with some of the top transformational speakers, authors and coaches throughout the world and most importantly, the gift of impacting thousands of lives across the globe. Who, because of my work, now live lives of health, wealth and freedom.

What I realized is that when I set out to be, do, and have more, the more possibilities I have in my life. The bigger I play, the more opportunities I have to live in my greatness. The more unstoppable I become, the more health, wealth and freedom I, my children and our world get to experience. So how dare I not live MORE life in order to avoid feeling uncomfortable. How selfish would I be if I allowed my comfort zone to keep me playing small? What would I look like allowing something that feels intimidating and scary to stop me from sharing my unique gifts with the world? I may be the only example someone has of being, doing and having more and I refuse to lay down on my life, or my responsibilities again. In this powerful book, Growth Coach Kimberly Buchanan lays down a simple-to-follow and easy-to-implement system for unlocking your potential. What I love most about Kim's approach is that it helps us identify that to **Be, Do,** and **Have**—we must first start by doing, accepting and taking on less. Though in unlocking your potential, you may find yourself in constant, massive action towards those roles and goals that are important to you, Kimberly shows us how to do this without feeling the need to live in overwhelm or be all things to all people.

Here's the truth... Unlocking your potential will require your uncommon application of the common knowledge shared within this book. So here is my charge to you: Do, apply and live the lessons and concepts in this book. Feel afraid and do it anyway. Feel uncomfortable and grow through it. Feel inadequate and require yourself to stretch. Be the superwoman that you already are, but be her for yourself. Watch what happens to your life as you begin to unlock your potential. Watch how your relationships improve as you become more intentional and selective in your choices and actions. Watch how your finances grow as you become more discriminating in your decisions and discerning about your priorities. Watch how your career, business and home-life flourishes as you begin living, loving and owning your divine assignment here on this planet.

INTRODUCTION

If you are reading this book, then you are a woman who is ready to make the changes necessary to **Be. Do.** and **Have More.** You are tired of deferring your dreams and multi-tasking just to keep your head above water, but never moving forward. Now is the time, whether you are a mid-level executive, entrepreneur, or a housewife, you feel a stirring. You know you could be something more than you are, and you are determined to become greater, do greater things, and therefore have more. Whether you want to have more time with your family, income, flexibility, or opportunities, this book can guide you toward unlocking your potential and having more of what you want in life.

It won't be easy. This plan for change includes 21 things to give up so you can grow. Seven years ago, I gave myself permission to **Be** all that I need to be in order to **Do** what moves me closer toward the things or the happiness I desire to **Have** in my life. And that wasn't solely based on my career. Sure, career was a factor in the things I wanted to be, do, and have; but today I realize that career was only one part of the equation. I had also desired balance and freedom in other areas of my life, too.

These are the 21 things to give up that I share with you throughout the pages of this book. This book is a powerful read with short lessons because I know you've got a busy life. I also included my Two, Three, and Me exercises at the conclusion of each chapter. These exercises are designed to help you learn two good ideas and make three real changes; plus reflect on yourself with a "me" exercise. As you read, you'll think about situations in your life, probably in a way you've never thought about them before. Embrace the process. Every woman deserves to **Be. Do.** and **Have More**, and you are no exception.

As you read on, please do me a favor. Find a nice, quiet location with minimal distractions as you read. I ask this because I want you to not just read words on paper, but to also think about what you are reading and how it applies to your life. Bring a pen with you, too. Reflect on your Two, Three, Me answers and make plans to apply them to your life today. Forgive yourself if you stumble at first. Although changes can be difficult at first, in time they will become as natural as brushing your teeth every morning. *Trust yourself.*

My JOURNEY

I recently looked at the calendar and felt amazed. I realized it had been seven years since I was last permanently employed by someone else. Seven years since I stopped working towards someone else's dream and started building my own. Seven years since I started putting myself and my goals first, versus trying to be "normal" or living the way I was expected to live. The seven-year anniversary had come and gone, without notice. During the years before, I was keenly aware of the anniversary.

What changed this year is simple. I've finally arrived. I've finally released the anger, guilt, and all the other negative emotions that followed when I decided to pursue my passion. Once I realized June 10th had come and gone like any other day, I was overjoyed and felt inspired. I reflected on how far I've come since releasing from my life all the baggage. That's when I decided to write about my journey and help other women unlock that same potential.

Today, I'm happy. I'm healthy. And I'm more financially stable than I've ever been. I have a clear vision and goals for the future. Each morning I wake up energized to work toward my goals. But most of all, I'm doing this work while being surrounded by my loving family and a support system and network that is necessary to sustain this level of elevation.

Today, I want to encourage you to do one thing: Give yourself permission to **Be. Do.** and **Have More.** That's it. Whatever your definition of "more" is... You deserve to have it. We all face limitations in life. But it is my sincere hope that you, as a woman, will recognize with razor-sharp accuracy exactly what is holding you back. And then, release the following 21 things from your life. By the time you finish reading this book, I know you'll have the power and the potential to do so.

Here's to **Being More. Doing More.** and **Having More.**

- Kimberly

KIMBERLYBUCHANAN.COM

| Not Being Honest About Past Mistakes |

> "Life's too short to lug around what ifs, regrets and disappointments."

KIMBERLYBUCHANAN.COM

1
NOT BEING HONEST ABOUT PAST MISTAKES

> *Be honest about your mistakes, learn the necessary lessons, and move forward.*

You probably already have ways to address problems that you recognize, but what do you do about the problems you can't or aren't willing to admit? Have you heard people say, "The first step to solving a problem is to admit there is a problem?" That can sound trite, but there's a reality to it. Whatever is not going right in your life, you can't fix it unless you admit it needs fixing.

On my way to **Be. Do.** and **Have More**, I had to step back for a reality check according to these problem-illuminating questions:

- *How come I'm not already there?*
- *Why haven't I reached my definition of "more" yet?*
- *What are some of the things that have and continue to stand in my way?*

You may be asking yourself, "Why does it matter as long as I'm ready to change now?" And yes, I've said on more than one occasion that you can start right where you are, you don't have to be perfect. I still stand by that. But I also believe that life's too short to lug around what ifs, regrets and disappointments. It's time to give those things up. You can do that by being honest about your past mistakes, learning the necessary lessons, and then moving forward.

I am on Team Dream, cheering you on, and I don't want you to make mistakes twice. If you aren't honest about the past, then you can't learn from it. One of the reasons why I was not making the money that most of my peers were making is because I made the mistake of not negotiating my first two contracts. I took whatever was given to me and walked away with it. Had I not gone back to understand this past mistake, I would have continued to be stuck. Learn from my mistakes, too!

Four Ways Successful People Are Honest About the Past to Make the Future Brighter

1. **Get clarity about what hasn't worked:** *Successful people go to the root of the problem and dissect it fully, tearing mistakes apart to get to the bottom of what happened to avoid it in the future.*

2. **Don't double-dip:** *Once successful people are clear about what has not worked, they don't do the same things, expecting different results. They either dummy-proof it or avoid it all together.*

3. **Make Sure It's Right for YOU:** *Successful people don't compromise. They ask themselves, "Should I be doing this?" "Is this the right time for this?" If it's not right, they don't do it.*

4. **Evaluate Now vs. Later:** *When making decisions, successful people weigh short-term fixes and long-term benefits. Often, the short-term fixes don't last and result in a loss of time and money.*

As you continue to unlock your potential, be sure you are clear about what has not worked in the past. Make sure the next step is right for you, while also evaluating the long-term benefits.

> "When making decisions, successful people weigh short-term fixes and long-term benefits."

TWO:
What are two past mistakes that you have ignored and not been honest about to learn from?

_____
_____
_____
_____
_____
_____
_____
_____
_____
_____
_____

THREE:
What three changes can you make to approach your past mistakes with a mindset of successful people?

_____
_____
_____
_____
_____
_____
_____
_____
_____
_____
_____

ME:
What will your life be like when you are learning from your mistakes instead of repeating them? Will those changes lead you to being more, doing more, having more, or all of the above?

_____
_____
_____
_____
_____
_____
_____
_____

| Not Using What You Have |

> "You already have what it takes."

2
NOT USING WHAT YOU HAVE

> *Don't undermine your God-given strengths, abilities, and talents because of fear or insecurity.*

So often women think, if I had more money, I could accomplish more. If I had a better job, I'd be happier. If I had more education, I could do something great. But as long as you feel as though you're lacking or shortchanged, you'll make more excuses to be less than you are destined to be.

You already have what it takes to be great. Don't undermine your God-given strengths, abilities, and talents because of fear or insecurity. Use your current talents or attributes, because that's how you will strengthen them. If there are areas where you need to improve, take this opportunity to study, get a certification, or take free courses online. Anything you can do to improve yourself and your well-being is another step towards your goal to **Be. Do.** and **Have More.** Do not accept excuses from yourself just because you're not where you want to be now or you will never get there.

Sheryl Sandberg said it best in her book, *Lean In*. Women need to shift from thinking, "I'm not ready to do that" to thinking "I want to do that—and I'll learn by doing."

When I first set out on my journey as an entrepreneur, I was thrown into the process. The fact is I was laid off from my corporate position. The "good" jobs were very scarce so I was forced to look at my current skill set and figure out a way to make money until I could find a permanent position. To my surprise, I'm still using my skills and talents as my primary source of income, seven years later. I got here by using what I had and building upon that foundation.

Here's what I know:

1. Everyone has a talent of some sort
2. Everyone has something that is unique about the skill set they possess
3. Everyone can use what they have as a way of getting to the goals they want to achieve. You may need to add on later, but what you have today is a means to get you started.

My friend Cindy was working in a C-level, corporate position. Her ultimate desire was to own a restaurant. At that particular time, she was not in a position to go into the restaurant business full time. She didn't know the first thing about running her own business or the food industry, but she knew she could cook and everyone around her validated that often. Cindy could have said, "It's just a passion, not a career," and let her dream die. But she didn't.

So, with the confidence in her cooking and no idea how to run a restaurant business, she began to use what she did have to get ahead.

1. Cindy was a numbers whiz: She started writing her recipes down on paper and determining exactly how much of the ingredients it would take to make them in larger quantities. From there, she researched and calculated costs for supplies, further breaking it down by the serving size per person.
2. She had a community: She held taste tests of the recipes in her nice, suburban home. Taste tests gradually included more and more people, so she could make her meals in large quantities and get even more good feedback from the people that might become customers.
3. She could learn: It took several months, but Cindy soon had a full menu that she was happy with. She did all of this while researching what it takes to run a successful restaurant business and receiving the food certifications required.

Think about the talents you're blessed with and start using them to move you towards doing more. If you have Cindy's #3, then everything else can be figured out, and I know you can learn. What else makes you special, that you can use to build your skill set, and do more of what you want to do?

> *Think about the talents you're blessed with and start using them to move you towards doing more.*

| Not Using What You Have |

TWO:
What are two skills you already have that you could be using to get ahead? Write them down.

_____
_____
_____
_____
_____
_____
_____
_____
_____
_____

THREE:
What three actions can you take now to use your unique talents and build your skill set?

_____
_____
_____
_____
_____
_____
_____
_____
_____
_____

ME:
How will it benefit you to use your skills and uplift your dream? How can this lead you to being more, doing more, having more, or all of the above?

_____
_____
_____
_____
_____
_____
_____
_____
_____

| Thinking Small |

> "Stop Limiting your own Options."

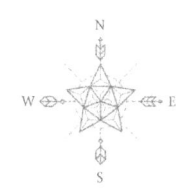

3
THINKING SMALL

> *Think beyond your wildest dreams and surround yourself with people who are making their dreams happen in a big way.*

I grew up in a town where most people had parents who worked at one of our local manufacturers. There was the gum factory, Chrysler, Kodak, an aerospace company, and another company that made beautiful accessories for the home. For many of my friends, their goal was to graduate high school and get one of those "good jobs."

When I finished college, I wanted to come back home and get one of those "good jobs," too. I started out pretty good. Within a few years, I was making more money than most adults and I was in my early 20's. My "good job" was at the aerospace company. It was a place that you could work and earn a good income for yourself and your family. After a few years, it fell apart and I was laid off. I moved on to another good company, and that blew up, too. I was laid off again.

From that point on, I went for the gusto. Following the last layoff, I couldn't find another "good job" and I made a decision to own my own business. For a woman in my small town, this was a BIG decision. I was going against the norm—very much against what I was "supposed" to do.

Unlock Your Potential

What I was supposed to do was collect the unemployment insurance until I could convince another one of those "good" companies to hire me.

I was a small fish in a little pond, coming from a city with 25,000 people, and I shifted my focus to nearby Chicago with 2.7 million people, where I was a smaller fish in a very big pond. I quickly learned that everything needed to change about the way I did business. I had to change the way I negotiated, the way I dressed, my demeanor, and even my conversation-style. People in Chicago move fast. Very seldom are they laid-back, so as a business woman I couldn't be, either.

Being in such a large pond, I learned the sky is the limit because I was around people who had big dreams and they were working to make it happen—and it was happening for them. They were making plans to grow and succeed. They had big goals and aspirations. I learned from their examples and started swimming like a bigger fish and thinking bigger.

I learned some things from swimming with the big fish that I would like to pass on to you:

- You are what you say you are, so speak boldly
- You can do what you say you will do
- Nothing and no one can hold you back when you stop limiting your own options

Think beyond your wildest dreams and surround yourself with people who are making their dreams happen in a big way. Don't settle for good enough because that's not a growth position, and if you stay there, you will remain vulnerable to changes outside your control. When you think big, there are still circumstances that can affect your outlook, but you will be in a much more empowered position to do what you need to do to keep moving forward. Remember you are not just capable of "good enough," but you are capable of real greatness when you think big.

> *Don't settle for good enough... if you stay there, you will remain vulnerable to changes outside your control.*

TWO:
What are the two most important things in your life that are "good enough"?

_____
_____
_____
_____
_____
_____
_____
_____
_____
_____

THREE:
What three changes can you make to surround yourself with more successful people and think bigger?

_____
_____
_____
_____
_____
_____
_____
_____
_____
_____

ME:
How will your life be better when you are swimming with bigger fish? How can that proximity lead you to being more, doing more, having more, or all of the above?

_____
_____
_____
_____
_____
_____
_____
_____

> "Improving your quality of life is neither offensive or wrong."

4
GUILT

> *Webster's Dictionary defines guilt as a feeling of responsibility or remorse for some offense, drive, wrong, etc., whether real or imagined.*

However, making decisions that will improve your quality of life does not match this definition, so why do we feel guilty for doing so? Making a decision to improve your quality of life is neither offensive or wrong. In other words, the guilt you feel for wanting to **Be. Do.** and **Have More.** is likely unproductive and misplaced. And yet for many of us, that guilt persists anyway.

Let's think about where it likely comes from. Often, this guilt sets in because you have other people who are depending on you to remain exactly as you are and provide exactly what you've been providing for years. Most likely, these people are family and friends. In thinking about making a change, you feel torn between wanting to do what you know is right for you and not rocking the boat with anyone you care about. You may also feel guilty because you can't take everyone with you on this journey. Someone is going to miss out on what you've been providing, even if it has frankly gone on too long.

For example, you might have started out with occasionally watching your sister's children, and now it has turned into watching them several times every week. And you are trying to figure out what you should do because you feel bad for letting your sister down. What you are feeling is normal. You are a kind person who cares about people, and that is a good trait. Don't get rid of that. But, until you start caring for yourself first, you can be of no assistance to anyone else. And once you are doing, being, and having more, you will have more to give, too. Feeling guilty for doing what you need to do to succeed is only looking at the short term.

I remember when I first started out on my journey. I needed to maximize my time and spend the necessary hours it was going to take to work on me. That means I needed to resign from serving on several community boards of directors. When I made the decision to pull back, I felt like I was letting so many people down. But something great happened as a result working on myself. A few years later, after meeting a few of my goals, I was able to start my own foundation, which will continue to fulfill my mission perhaps even more than serving on the community boards.

Over time, you feel better about putting yourself first and see the benefits to the extent that you know by helping yourself you are helping your friends and family even more. After that initial investment in yourself, you get a sense of that good, growth feeling which leads to investing more often, and soon it becomes constant.

So that's where we are today. You are making that initial investment on paying yourself first in terms of investing in your growth first. And it's okay. Feeling guilty about it is counterproductive; instead of feeling guilty, take this time as an opportunity to note your experiences on your journey. When you've reached your goals, use your notes as a reference to help someone else along the way. That's another way your growth can help people you care about.

> *After that initial investment in yourself, you get a sense of that good, growth feeling which leads to investing more often, and soon it becomes constant.*

TWO:
What are the two situations in your life that make you feel guilty? Write them down.

_____
_____
_____
_____
_____
_____
_____
_____
_____
_____
_____

THREE:
What three actions can you take now to change those patterns of guilt and put yourself first?

_____
_____
_____
_____
_____
_____
_____
_____
_____
_____
_____

ME:
How is getting rid of this guilt going to help you in the future? What changes could happen to lead you to being more, doing more, having more, or all of the above?

_____
_____
_____
_____
_____
_____
_____
_____
_____
_____

| Saying Yes To Everything |

> "Set boundaries and ensure those around you adhere to them."

KIMBERLYBUCHANAN.COM

5
SAYING YES TO EVERYTHING

"You can't be everything to everybody."

Y ou can't move very far if you are crazy busy with everyone else's problems. Set boundaries and ensure those around you are adhering to them. Otherwise, you run the risk of getting completely off track. But I bet I didn't have to tell you that. You can't be everything to everybody.

Early-on, I enjoyed having people come to me for assistance. Although I had no doubt that I was smart and resourceful, it made me feel good when someone else validated those feelings by asking me to do something for them. I took on everything I was asked to do, from planning parties to graphic design to typing resumes. You name it, I was the go-to-person for my family and friends. Before I knew it, I was spending hours and sometimes days on other people's projects. I bet you can relate. Soon, I began to push things I needed to get done for myself farther and farther down my list. By the time I was able to get to some of the things I needed to have done, it was late at night and I was exhausted. That didn't work for me.

I love my family and I love my friends, of course, and I didn't completely stop helping them out. But I did make a pact with myself to think first before saying "yes." I invite you to use this thought process as your guide to only do what you should be doing.

The next time someone asks you to do something, be slow to speak. Ask yourself these three questions:

1. *How much time is this going to take?*
2. *Do I currently have that time available to give to someone else?*
3. *If yes: How am I going to respond?*
   If no: How am I going to respond?

Let's begin with #1: How much time is this going to take? When asking yourself this question, focus on the deliverable, or what is it that you need to hand over to this person. The second thing is to break that deliverable down into parts, so you are aware of everything involved with saying "yes." Then, put a time limit on each part of the deliverable. The goal is to determine, to a fixed number of minutes or hours, how much time is required to complete the tasks. Then you can determine if it's worth it to you to give this much of your time to this request.

Number #2: Once you know how much time the task is going to take, look at your calendar to determine if that amount of time is available. In other words, is it even within your ability to give the amount of time the task requires? And if it is vacant, do you want to fill that time with this particular task? Be honest. You don't have to do anything you don't want to do.

If yes, your response should be:
I have ____ (number of hours) to help you out on (insert particular date). If this does not work for you, I'm afraid I can't assist you.

If no, your response should be:
I'm sorry. I wish I could help you. But looking at my calendar for the week/month, I do not have anywhere to fit this in. However, I do have someone/something I can recommend to help you."

These are examples of how to say yes, with boundaries, and how to say no while letting people know you still care.

TWO:
What are the two most important things you need to quit saying yes to doing? Write them down.

_____
_____
_____
_____
_____
_____
_____
_____
_____
_____

THREE:
What three actions can you take to stop saying yes to everything?

_____
_____
_____
_____
_____
_____
_____
_____
_____
_____

ME:
How will not saying yes when you don't want to benefit you? How will your actions lead you to being more, doing more, having more, or all of the above?

_____
_____
_____
_____
_____
_____
_____
_____
_____

| Wearing Your Heart On Your Sleeve |

> "Strike a *Balance* between being your kind self & keeping yourself *Protected*."

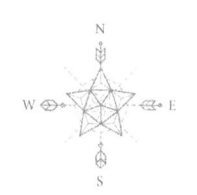

6
WEARING YOUR HEART ON YOUR SLEEVE

> *How DO you strike a balance between being your kind self and keeping yourself protected?*

You are a nice person, right? So logically, you would think the people you encounter should be nice as well. In life, this is not always true. And sometimes, especially when you already feel vulnerable, being ill-treated can be a very hard pill to swallow. These things will happen: harsh comments, constant refusals, being taken for granted, being left off a guest list, and the list goes on. So, let's see how you can strike a balance between being your kind self and keeping yourself protected.

I've always tried to base my decisions on doing the most good and putting only things out there that I think people, especially women, can benefit from. This has been volunteering, serving on boards, and projects like this book. So, imagine my surprise when I began to encounter people who didn't care much about what I stand for. I was confused at first. And I thought, "What is there to NOT like about what I have to offer?" As you can see, I was too worried about whether they liked me and took it personally that they didn't want to join with me. This is no way to hold a bake sale, and it certainly won't help in your professional life.

So, I became curious. After I surveyed women, whom I believed liked what I offered, I realized that some women who are at certain points in their lives do not have a need for what I offer. It's nothing personal against me, it's just that they do not have the problem that I'm trying to solve. When they tell me "no," they are not telling me that there's no value in my services or any other kind of negative self-talk that we can tell ourselves. They only mean that it's not for them, at least not now. If she doesn't want to attend my fundraising gala, it's okay. However, I must be in a mindset to listen and really hear people so I can understand this kind of "no" and not be confused that it's about me and not their lack of need for what I am doing.

Everyone does not have to like what you offer, no matter what it is. You can't take that personally and be hurt every time someone says no. Now, when the person you want to help starts to not like what you offer, you may have a bit of a problem that needs to be fixed. For example, maybe people who want to support my gala think the tickets are too high, so maybe I picked the wrong venue with high fees. That's a real problem with a solution that has nothing to do with the cause or with me.

At other times, you may not have defined whom you are trying to reach in a narrow way. Step back, take a moment to define who you are speaking to, identify the problem(s) you can solve for them, and then put yourself out there and let them know who you are. You only need those people to like you, and that's going to be a narrow niche of people who should be drawn to you. Who needs and will value your leadership, skills, or expertise?

I learned early-on that whether I am building relationships in business or with other parents at my son's school, I need to know who I am looking for, in order to avoid getting hurt by trying to be liked by people who are just wrong for me. I developed this list of three questions so when I meet new people, I don't wear my heart on my sleeve and instead gravitate toward like-minded individuals:

Who seems naturally attracted to you?
Who are you excited to serve?
Who can and will give real support to your mission?

Once you can answer these questions, look back at times your feelings were hurt because you thought someone didn't like you and ask yourself if they were even your ideal relationship. Most likely, they weren't, and that should help you feel better and take the criticism with a grain of salt as you move forward. If someone doesn't agree with what you stand for or need what you're promoting, they wouldn't accept it if it was free. That's just fine. You should like them anyway and move on to serve the people who need you and want to help you. In this way, you unlock your potential.

TWO:
Think of two times your feelings got hurt because someone said no to you. What might have been the reason they said no, which had nothing to do with you personally?

_____
_____
_____
_____
_____
_____
_____
_____
_____
_____

THREE:
What three things can you change about the way you look for people to join your mission to unlock your potential, so you will better target likeminded people?

_____
_____
_____
_____
_____
_____
_____
_____
_____

ME:
What will improve in your life when you start being okay with hearing no? How will that help you to Be, Do, and Have More?

_____
_____
_____
_____
_____
_____
_____
_____
_____
_____

| Pleasing Others |

> "Shine from the inside out."

7
PLEASING OTHERS

> *Fill your cheering section with people you can learn from and those who support your needs when times get tough.*

Someone once said that everyone in the audience will not be clapping and cheering for you as you run your race in life, and that may have some truth to it. But I would add that if you are running in the direction of your cheering fan just to keep their approval and attention, that's going to get old and feel hollow sooner or later. Instead of doing what you think will please others, let's make time for you to assemble a new cheering section. Let's make this one filled with people who are perfectly fine with who you are and what you desire for your life. Fill your cheering section with people you can learn from and those who support your needs when times get tough.

I know a lot about how to do this the right way and the wrong way. This takes me back to my high school days. Everyone wants to please their parents and family, right? I originally went to college to study communications. I told everyone I was going to be a news anchor on the local evening news, which made my family excited for me. Looking back, I can now say that I wanted to be a news anchor because of what it looks like to the outside vs. what the job really entails. I came to a point when I had to risk disappointing my cheering section and change my course. Then I found out who my loyal fans were, who stayed with me because they wished me well.

That same sense of wanting to belong and to please others followed me into my career. Once I got into my profession, I longed for a nice office and a VP title. My cheering section approved. Once I reached that milestone, it was not what I expected. I went for the job, thinking it was the next step in my career progression, something I was supposed to do and something that would look great to other people when they asked for my business card or saw the VP title under my email signature.

Since that time, I've learned that the only person you need to please is yourself. We all have certain people in our lives who we want to please. This might be your family, your spouse, your children, your colleagues, and even your bosses or mentors. But the best way to make an impact on others is to be your true, authentic self.

Shine from the inside out, not from the outside in.

You'll know your loyal fans because they will be cheering you on whether you are chasing a glamorous goal or pulling back to take care of yourself. Most of all, when you are doing what you want to be doing, you will become your own cheering section, and outside validation won't be nearly as important as the validation you give yourself.

What are some of the actions you've taken to please others instead of pleasing yourself? How did it make you feel to do what made them happy instead of doing what you really wanted to do? Think of one thing you are doing now just because it gets you approval. What would you do instead if you could? Find out what that is, and then give yourself permission to try it. It's that easy once you get started.

When you are running a race you care about, you'll find that you have more energy that comes from within, and soon you'll be crossing the finish lines that you set, not those imposed by others. And those are the most glorious wins of all.

> "You'll know your loyal fans because they will be cheering you on whether you are chasing a glamorous goal or pulling back to take care of yourself."

| Pleasing Others |

TWO:
Who are two of your loyal fans who want you to succeed as you define your success?

THREE:
What three things can you do to surround yourself with more successful and encouraging people?

ME:
How is getting negative people out of your cheering section going to benefit you? How will this lead you to being more, doing more, having more, or all of the above?

| Not Asking For Help |

> "Multi-tasking on micro-issues **prevents** you from **progressing**."

KIMBERLYBUCHANAN.COM

8
NOT ASKING FOR HELP

You're a one-woman-show who performs amazing feats and has for many years.

Wouldn't it be nice to be a superwoman? You probably are one already. You're a one-woman-show who performs amazing feats and has for many years. Between work and home, you are the CEO, accountant, marketing director, cook, secretary, and much more. Companies are asking executives to be more "lean," so businesses are cross-training employees to perform more than one job. Doing more with less is the way of the world, whether you are operating as an executive or a stay-at-home mom. And through it all, we are getting worse and worse at feeling able to ask for help.

What I learned from trying to do it all, without asking for help, is that overwhelm can result in unrelenting stress. For some reason, I felt like everything would not be done thoroughly and properly unless I did it myself. Sound familiar? When I was trying to do everything by myself, I was resentful and isolated, which made it even harder for anyone to offer help if they wanted to. I was performing routine tasks that were taking too much time and not providing any opportunity for me to develop in other areas that were important. In other words, I was multi-tasking on micro-issues, which prevented me from making progress on the big picture.

Finally, I was so stressed out and disappointed in my progress that I addressed my problem and took on the art of delegation. Yes, delegation. Instead of asking for help, as though I am incapable of doing something, I delegate and empower the person I call upon to do the job well. When you ask someone to do something in a way that makes them feel important and valued, they are more likely to do the job well and even appreciate being asked.

Every woman, whether you are an executive, entrepreneur, or stay-at-home mom, should take a hard look at all the things you currently have on your plate and start delegating those things that can be done by someone other than you. This will free up your time to make yourself more of a priority and make sure you are doing the things that really should be done by only you.

Here's a great sorting method I learned to make sure you keep doing the things you should do and delegate the rest. Make a list of everything you do every day, and then put a K for keep or a D for delegate beside each one.

> **KEEP:** The things you love doing, as well as those things that only you can do. Keep tending your flower beds if you love them, but maybe someone else can mow the lawn. Or maybe you need to do specialized tasks at work but can delegate business administration tasks. You may need to also keep, but only on a temporary basis, some of the things you do not enjoy but don't have anyone to delegate those things to. Keep your eyes open for a solution to the temporary keeps.

> **DELEGATE:** The things you do not enjoy, but other people find enjoyable. I have a friend who hates grocery shopping, and it turns out that her husband loves to grocery shop, so she delegated. Also, delegate things you enjoy, but have already mastered, and in this way, you help your family or staff develop new skills. Yes, you can write your blogs, but wouldn't it be great if your assistant could write them just as well and free up your time?

The goal is for you to be doing only the things that bring you enjoyment or use your specialized skills. This will leave you with enough spare time to develop new skills and interests that will give you satisfaction and pride so you can keep moving forward and not be trapped in the stress of trying to do everything all by yourself. That's no fun and not the way to **Be. Do.** and **Have More.**

> *"Every woman should take a hard look at all the things you currently have on your plate and start delegating."*

TWO:
What two things are holding you back from asking for help when you need it?

_____
_____
_____
_____
_____
_____
_____
_____
_____
_____

THREE:
List at least three things you plan to delegate in order to free up your time to work on yourself.

_____
_____
_____
_____
_____
_____
_____
_____
_____
_____

ME:
How is this going to benefit you when you're finished taking action? Will this change lead you to being more, doing more, having more, or all of the above?

_____
_____
_____
_____
_____
_____
_____
_____
_____

| Drags And Weights |

> "Free Yourself and Rise to Greatness."

9
DRAGS AND WEIGHTS

> *Figure out who's dragging you down.*

This is where it gets real. If there are people in your life close to you, and they aren't caring, supportive, or even a little bit interested in what's important to you, then you may want to add them to Team Toxic instead of Team Dream.

Here's a tool I adapted from Joel Osteen that I use to decide what kinds of people are around me. We will use NASA's four forces that impact an airplane's speed, altitude, and orientation, and use the same process to evaluate the people in your life to find out if they are forces for growth or not. Those four forces are: THE DRAG, THE WEIGHT, THE THRUST, and THE LIFT. Don't worry, this is not going to be overly technical, and it's very helpful.

The reality is—The airplane only rises if the lift is greater than the weight. Consequently, the plane will begin to fall if the weight is greater than the lift. Looking at the drag and the thrust, the plane slows if the drag is greater than the thrust, but it accelerates when the thrust is greater than the drag. Understanding this concept, let's apply it metaphorically to the people in your life. Imagine that you are the plane. Who are your drags, weights, thrusters, and lifters?

Team Toxic: Weights and Drags

Drags are people that don't necessarily contribute anything to your team. They're simply holding on to you. You can't turn to them for advice or help. Why? Because they're always depending on you, but you can never depend on them to be there for you when you need them. Weights CAN NOT accept your growth. They want to hold you down and hold you back. These people are always very negative. When you tell them your plans, they start pointing out what can't be done. They don't want to see you get a new promotion at work or a nicer home for your family.

Team Dream: Thrusters and Lifters

Now we're getting to the good part, the **Thrusters**. These are people on your team that push you forward, not backward. They thrust you in the right direction and help keep you going, no matter what their current circumstances are. You can put your trust in your Thrusters. And finally, you have **Lifters**. These are people that encourage you, brighten your spirits during tough times in life, and they're also there to help you celebrate and give you praise during the happy times.

You want to surround yourself with your Lifters and Thrusters so you are continuously moving forward, lifting to even greater heights. Sometimes, when you are trying to reach a goal or a milestone, it gets tough. It can be frustrating and sometimes you feel like giving up. Having the right people around you will be key.

It's disappointing to discover that family members and close friends are drags or weights. Before you get all soft on me, I want to be clear that you do not have to stop loving these people. But DO be mindful of what you can and cannot share with them—in both conversations and in experience.

For example, if Thelma resents your desire to move from the not-so-great neighborhood both of you grew up and lived in for 20-plus years, then Thelma isn't the friend to discuss your moving plans with or take to open houses. You can speak together, but not about you leaving the neighborhood.

> *Who's on your Dream Team? Let's take a moment to identify them.*

TWO:
Identify at least two people who are drags and two people who are weights in your life.

_____
_____
_____
_____
_____
_____
_____
_____
_____
_____

THREE:
Identify at least three people who can lift you up and three who can thrust you forward:

_____
_____
_____
_____
_____
_____
_____
_____
_____
_____

ME:
Write this down: *I commit to myself that I will call on my lifters and thrusters the next time I'm going through the following circumstances.* Then, take your list of lifters and thrusters and add their numbers and email addresses so you have them in reach:

_____
_____
_____
_____
_____
_____
_____

| Being Scared To Put Yourself Out There |

> "Be around people who are more accomplished."

10
BEING SCARED TO PUT YOURSELF OUT THERE

> *Your network is your net worth.*

Your network is your net worth. I can't say that enough. Once you step up your game and start being around people who are more accomplished than you, you become challenged to **Be. Do.** and **Have More.**

My great friend CeCe once said, "For now, you need to get comfortable with being uncomfortable." I'd like to pass this same advice on to you. What CeCe meant by this statement is that once you set out on your way being more, you'll need to give yourself time to settle into your new and improved self. So, don't expect it to feel natural at first. Getting comfortable with meeting successful people will not happen overnight. It may be a little uncomfortable at first, but once you start seeing the results from making these connections, you'll quickly settle into your new normal as a professional networker.

Years ago, the main thing holding me back from networking was fear, and it holds a lot of other women back, too. I was afraid that I would need to talk about myself to other people. And yes, I was going to have to do just that. I was also afraid that in helping others get to know more about me, I would have to reveal my values and my skill set. I've always been a private person, so the thought of coming out of my shell horrified me. I didn't understand why it scared me so badly. I needed to get to the root of the problem.

I started by thinking about what made me uncomfortable about speaking about myself. I identified the following as my top three fears:

1. Fear of being put on the spot
2. Fear of not knowing what to say
3. Fear of saying the wrong things, whenever I did decide to speak

My solution to this problem allowed me to finally step outside my comfort zone.

And it's simple.

Identify your strengths, great qualities about yourself, and the things that make you unique. Then, you'll have something to talk about without thinking too hard. Be ready to state your name, position, and firm with pride. Practice with a friend or a mirror and get good at saying a sentence or two about the things you do that you love the most. When you know what you are going to say, you will approach networking with confidence.

Also, think of the questions you can ask others. You can reduce the pressure you feel to sell yourself when you instead focus your energy on learning about the people you meet. Ask questions that you want to be asked, and you will be creating your own comfortable environment. "What's your business?" "What a great speaker! What did you learn?" and "I don't think we've met yet, tell me about yourself" are great ways to break the ice and build relationships.

Walking into a situation where you have something you know you can talk about makes all the difference. For me, this transformed the way I felt when networking, competing for corporate contracts, speaking to groups, and other new opportunities to put myself out there.

As you are on your journey to **Be. Do.** and **Have More.**, don't let fear of speaking about yourself cause you to miss opportunities. Stop to think about the things that make you uncomfortable and how these things are holding you back from your definition of "more." Once you know what you're afraid of, you have the power to change it.

> *On your journey to Be. Do. and Have More, don't let fear of speaking about yourself cause you to miss opportunities.*

TWO:
What are two fears that are holding you back from putting yourself out there?

_____
_____
_____
_____
_____
_____
_____
_____
_____
_____

THREE:
What three actions will you take to start networking and telling others about yourself?

_____
_____
_____
_____
_____
_____
_____
_____
_____
_____

ME:
How is being able to speak about yourself going to benefit your goals? How will this change lead you to being more, doing more, having more, or all of the above?

_____
_____
_____
_____
_____
_____
_____
_____

> "Quit listening to speak and instead Listen to Understand."

11
TALKING INSTEAD OF LISTENING

"You can say the same sentence with different inflections and create completely different meanings."

When I first arrived in Chicago, I thought I needed to talk a lot to prove that I knew my business. I thought I needed to let people know that I belonged in their circle. I would sit in meetings with top executives, and instead of listening to understand them, I was listening for my chance to reply, comment, ask a question—anything to talk. I was listening to the smallest details they would mention to comment on them, instead of understanding the big picture. In short, I was sabotaging myself by talking too much and not listening.

One day, I was speaking with someone at the firm, and out of a random conversation, I asked, "What do you think I need to improve on around here?" He said to me, "As a consultant, you need to listen a bit more. We know you know your stuff, that's why we have you here. But we want to ensure you understand the big picture so please, let us explain our version of it to you before you respond."

Talk about a wake-up call.

From that point on, I opened myself up by being a "fly on the wall." Now, when I do decide to speak, it is to share meaningful information. And because I do not speak as often as others, people tend to stop and listen when I do have something to say.

I encourage you to pay close attention to not only your verbal but also your non-verbal speaking habits. What you say—how you say it—and when you say it—are very important. You want people to view you as trustworthy, credible, and confident. When they view you that way, they tend to believe in your message. You can say the same sentence with different inflections and create completely different meanings. For instance, if the man who gave me the honest feedback had made his voice higher or spoken quickly, I might have thought he was upset and taken what he said more personally.

Also, watch your nonverbal communication. Posture and eye contact are two components that can trip you up if you're not aware of the effect you might be having on others. Not making eye contact while others are speaking might make them think you're not listening, and sitting with your arms crossed can seem hostile or at least like you are closed off and not willing to engage, which is rarely helpful. In contrast, making eye contact and nodding occasionally shows that you are following the conversation without saying a word. You can also keep your arms open to show that you are open to receiving what they have to say to you.

Learning to listen vs. talk can help you not only in the work place but in personal relationships as well. My husband and children have appreciated my willingness to hear them out, and understand the big picture. It has cut down on many misunderstandings and disagreements at home as well as in business.

The next time you are in a meeting, notice if you listen more or talk more. What are the communication behaviors of the people around you? You'll probably notice that the people who make the biggest impact are not the ones who do all the talking, but the ones who actively listen and have the best understanding of the full discussion. When you quit listening to speak and instead listen to understand, you will find ways to **Be. Do.** and **Have More.**

> *Making eye contact and nodding occasionally shows that you are following the conversation without saying a word.*

TWO:
What are two relationships you can improve by listening more and speaking less?

_____
_____
_____
_____
_____
_____
_____
_____
_____

THREE:
What three things are you going to watch for in your nonverbal communication to make sure you are speaking in the way you want to be received?

_____
_____
_____
_____
_____
_____
_____
_____
_____

ME:
How is improving your listening skills going to help you succeed more? How can these changes lead you to being more, doing more, having more, or all of the above?

_____
_____
_____
_____
_____
_____
_____

| Impatience |

> "Every small Step or Milestone is a victory."

12
IMPATIENCE

> *Find ways to Grow Where You Are.*

You want change. You want results. And you want them to happen RIGHT NOW, right? When change doesn't happen as quickly as you would like, you sometimes stop trying.

Impatience is an awkward issue to address. We've all been to that point of being totally done! I know I have. I recall traveling to a client's office several days a week, four hours round-trip, often in snow storms. The commute was brutal. I would sometimes pull over to the side of the road because the streets were a complete white-out, and I couldn't see two feet in front of me. As I sat in my car, I would often think to myself, "This is never going to end. I've been on the road for two years now and I really can't see any type of end-point." My life felt like I was trapped in a snow storm, and I was impatient for springtime. Sound familiar?

The logical answer would be to find another job, right? But sometimes when we have other responsibilities it's not exactly that easy and you must find ways to **Grow Where You Are**. If it was so easy, then we would all be doing it automatically. I needed to learn to find peace in the storm and make small changes toward a bigger goal. It wasn't until I started to set goals and forecast small milestones that I started to see a way out.

One day I sat down and asked myself the following three questions:

1. What is your ultimate goal?
2. What do you need to make this happen?
3. What are some small steps you can take right now to move in that direction?

Once I answered the three questions, I developed smart, focused goals. The first milestone I conquered was to evaluate every task I did on the job that I could perform from my home office. After that, I moved on to count the actual number of face-to-face meetings vs. conference calls on any given day. Armed with the data I needed, I set out to make myself invaluable. I took on tasks that could only be performed by me, so the "higher-ups" could see the value I brought to the table. Then, it was time to strike. I asked to work two days virtually and three days in the office. Once I showed how well that went for everyone, I moved up to asking to work more days from home. I was armed with data to prove that I could still do the job successfully.

The job I just described launched me into working several other contracts for Fortune 500 companies, which were all now 100% completed from the comfort of my home office. I needed to be able to successfully work from home on one project, then receive great reference letters from my high-powered client, and from there, I could show other companies that I had the skills to get the job done--virtually. I often wonder where I would be, had I quit when things turned a little rough, instead of finding a solution. I know that I would have missed many opportunities that followed.

Patience is a key attribute if you want to BE all that you need to be to DO what moves you closer toward the things or the happiness you desire to HAVE in your life. Every small step or milestone is a victory.

> *Patience is a key attribute if you want to BE all that you need to be ...*

TWO:
What are two problems you are impatient to solve?

_____
_____
_____
_____
_____
_____
_____
_____
_____
_____

THREE:
What three steps can you take to move yourself in the ultimate direction of your goals?

_____
_____
_____
_____
_____
_____
_____
_____
_____
_____

ME:
How will being patient allow you to approach your goals more strategically? Will these changes lead you to being more, doing more, having more or all of the above?

_____
_____
_____
_____
_____
_____
_____
_____
_____

| Distractions |

> "Remove everything that does not align"

13
DISTRACTIONS

> *Now is the time to set a strong focus on your priorities.*

Social media, emails, and numerous other things can become distractions from our plans to **Be**, **Do**, and **Have More**. Now is the time to remove everything from your life that does not align with the life you are trying to live. Now is the time to set a strong focus on your priorities. Make everything you do productive, working toward what you're trying to accomplish. Anything else should go!

Two of the main culprits for me were emails and social media. Until I started limiting myself, I hadn't really realized how big a distraction they were. Screens were robbing me of my current reality, and even my happiness. Sounds harsh, huh? But it's true and here's why: **TIME**.

Yes, time. The first thing I did, upon waking in the morning, was check my email. Big mistake! Ideally, you want to be proactive and in control during the first part of your day. You want to be in charge and set the tone. Chances are, there are one or two emails in your inbox that stand a chance of altering your mood and taking over your day before it even starts. I learned this valuable information from Julie Morgenstern's *Organizing from the Inside Out*.

After checking email, I would spend 10-15 minutes scrolling through Facebook and Instagram. From there, I checked my emails again. But it didn't stop there.

Throughout the day, I stopped to give my attention to the computer every single time it alerted me to a new email. The same goes for every text message. I checked Facebook and email several times throughout the day. I was caught up in who's posted something new, liked my posts, read my blogs, etc. I'd stop to check these things right in the middle of important projects that I needed to complete.

One of my clients provided me information about this topic to break my distraction. Did you know research shows that office workers are interrupted every eight minutes? To make things worse, the impact of each distraction is two or three times the length of time of the distraction. In other words, one hour of uninterrupted work is equivalent to three or four hours of productive time with interruptions.

Fortunately, there's an easy fix for these digital distractions. If you open your inbox four times per day, at set times, you will have much more control of your day and won't miss anything important. Schedule uninterrupted time each day to process email. Read items only once and either answer, delete, or move to a specific folder to archive them. You can also model good email etiquette to make sure your emails aren't distracting others, too.

Follow these tips when sending emails:

1. Be brief
2. Write a clear subject line
3. Do not Reply All unless it is absolutely necessary
(otherwise the conversation could drag on)

Sometimes the distractions are also in person. Set boundaries with co-workers and even your boss not to interrupt your work and give them windows when you are open to take questions or speak with them. Make sure they know it's so you will be more productive! Everyone on the team wins when you accomplish more in a shorter amount of time. Remove distractions from your daily life and you'll discover more time than you can imagine to **Be. Do.** and **Have More.**

> *Everyone on the team wins when you accomplish more in a shorter amount of time.*

TWO:
What two distractions are preventing you from focusing on your tasks?

THREE:
What three changes can you make to your approach to electronic communication to stop letting it control you?

ME:
How will you benefit from not letting emails and social media distract you? How will this lead you to being more, doing more, having more, or all of the above?

| Social Media |

> "Everyone is not who they 'Post' to be."

14
SOCIAL MEDIA

A good rule of thumb is limit your time on social media. When time is up, log out.

Sometimes, you need to re-establish control over the social media or else it can start to control you. I started to experience some of this and that's why I've had to give it up, several times, while on my journey to **Be. Do.** and **Have More**.

When engaged in social media you are constantly reminded of other people's accomplishments and other people's problems, too. When constantly engaged, you become focused on other people instead of being focused on yourself. Most likely, this happens without you being conscious of it.

What do you do when someone posts an accomplishment? You probably feel obligated to either comment or let them know you care; or you start to evaluate where you are in comparison to them, right? It's a slippery slope. And then, when someone posts a problem or something sad, what do you do? You might start to feel bad for them or think about how you can help them, right? In this way, your happiness is dependent on what other people decide to post. I've seen things on social media that have altered my entire week, and that is not helpful to me or them in any way.

The reality is, more than half of the people you are connected with on social media are not even acquaintances. You are only connected to them through this specific technology. Outside of that, you have no connection. And let's face it, you don't even personally know a lot of the people you are connected to, which is all the more reason why you should let it go and focus on yourself; or limit your interaction and investment with online relationships. Everyone is not who they "post" to be, anyway.

A good rule of thumb is to limit your time on social media. When time is up, log out, regardless of what you have not had a chance to sift through. In this way, you re-establish control over how your day is going. And if you must remain logged in and can't give it up, start using social media wisely and do not let it take up your precious time when you know you have other things that are more of a priority. Turn your notifications off so you won't be interrupted from other work just because your sister-in-law posted a recipe and tagged you.

When I first got into social media, I connected with anyone who wanted to connect with me. I joined any network that invited me to join. But then, when I began my journey to **Be. Do.** and **Have More**, all of that changed.

I went cold turkey from all social media for a bit, and I'll do it again if I feel that it's taking too much of my time again. Today, I use social media in a more productive way. It has become a tool for me, and I use it in accordance with a plan that compliments the life I desire to live. I connect with the people that make sense for me to be connected with. I share things that are related to my brand and who I desire to be as a mom, wife, Christian, and business woman.

Here's what I suggest you do. Take a break from social media for 30 days. Notice how you use your time instead. Once you go back, if you decide to reconnect, change your habits to be more strategically connected and maximize the relationships you want to nurture.

> *Don't let Social Media control you.*
> *YOU control Social Media.*

TWO:
What two things could you do with the time you spend on social media?

_____
_____
_____
_____
_____
_____
_____
_____
_____
_____

THREE:
What three things can you do now to limit your social media exposure?

_____
_____
_____
_____
_____
_____
_____
_____
_____
_____

ME:
What will be different in your life when you control your social media engagement? How can these changes lead you to being more, doing more, having more, or all of the above?

_____
_____
_____
_____
_____
_____
_____
_____
_____

| Unhealthy Habits |

> "Understand what you need to be at Peak Performance,"

KIMBERLYBUCHANAN.COM

15
UNHEALTHY HABITS

> *Knowing what your body requires, and the unhealthy habits you need to let go of, are essential.*

Are you productive, healthy and happy on eight hours of sleep? Does it take only seven hours of sleep to ensure you reach peak performance all day long? Do you have health issues such as being overweight? Are you at risk for any diseases? Do you depend on caffeine to get through the day? Are you paying attention to your individual needs by assessing how you feel on different amounts of sleep? According to the National Sleep Foundation, these are some of the questions you should be asking yourself because not getting enough sleep is a common unhealthy habit.

It all changed for me when I noticed I was gaining weight and getting very sleepy around 2:00 pm every day. It was also hard to maintain a healthy weight when visiting client's offices nearly every day. When boredom set in, I would bounce over to a co-worker's desk to visit the community candy jar in her cubicle. This would happen at least 2-3 times per day. Plus, there were weekly birthday donuts and other treats on hand. I worked a lot in the pharmaceutical industry, which is notorious for 3-4 meetings per day, all with rich foods.

Unfortunately, the weight gain led to high blood pressure. The high blood pressure, which was all-new to me, led to stress. The stress made my sleep poor. The inability to sleep led to low performance on the job. Low performance and worry about the status of my contracts, led to stress and attitude at home. You see the ripple effect? This all happened in a matter of six months.

Once you take control of your body and understand the signs, you can better understand what you need to be at peak performance to reach your goals throughout the day. For me, I need 6-7 hours of sleep at night. A light breakfast is fine for me. Lunch is essential. And dinner before 7 pm is essential. One or two cups of coffee is my maximum per day. Some exercise, at least 2-3 days a week, keeps me where I need to be physically, and I feel good.

Knowing what your body requires, and the unhealthy habits you need to let go of, are essential. I found that the most successful people stick to a ritual. They wake up at the same time every day, they maintain an exercise routine, and many of them take time out their day to meditate.

What I found interesting, and what prompted me to write my e-book, titled *"Morning Rituals: How Highly Successful People Start Their Days,"* is that successful women make it a habit to maintain routines. When you know what to expect from your day, simple things become enjoyable. Happy women also look for good things taking place around them; people smiling, the opportunity to lift someone else up, healthy conversations.

Here's a list to get you started on your new, healthier habits:

1. *Get proper rest*
2. *Rise and dine*
3. *Move your body*
4. *Empower yourself to be the very best you.*

Sometimes it takes years of being an adult to get the confidence and self-worth you need to power through anything that gets in your way. But once you develop it, you must stay in that space. The only way to stay there is to constantly remind yourself of how great you are – and to remember to treat yourself as you should.

> *When you know what to expect from your day, simple things become enjoyable.*

TWO:
What are the two healthy changes you can make to your daily routine?

THREE:
What are three areas of opportunity where you can see your health suffering because of your work habits?

ME:
How is your life going to improve with your new healthy habits? How will they lead you to being more, doing more, having more or all of the above?

| Control |

> "Be prepared to Loosen your tight Grip on the Reins."

16
CONTROL

> *Allow people into your life that can help you reach your goals.*

Control. **That's a big word!** According to Merriam-Webster, it means "to have power over." Well, guess what, in an effort to **Be. Do.** and **Have More**, you're going to need to release your tight control on things and allow influential, successful people into your life that can help you.

Until I decided to transition in a direction that allows me to have more, I had never considered a coach or a mentor. Today, I have a few of them in my life. There's a difference between a mentor and a coach. I had a mentor in my corporate career and have had a few coaches within my seven-year journey as a business owner, who have turned into some of my closest friends.

Mentors: Found more in the corporate world and they help people chart out their career path, either within the same company or outside. Mentors are usually senior level people who have moved up through the ranks. Mentees are usually new or mid-level managers who are planning their goals for the next 5-10 years out (mentoring is long-term). They want to enhance their skills and build relationships to move to the next level. They're trying to take their current assignments and leverage them for upward mobility.

As a Mentee your goals should be to:

- Expand professional and personal networks
- Learn about different career paths
- Increase self-awareness
- Gain support in a current or new role

You'll notice that mentoring is relationship and development driven. Both mentors and mentees benefit because it involves both the professional and the personal. It's transformational and requires a safe environment where you can share things that involve your self-confidence, self-perception, etc.

Coaches: Coaching is a short-term relationship, with a specific goal in mind. You know where you are trying to go, you just need a design and a plan to get there and you are looking for a subject-matter expert to help you. Noticed I said expert. That means someone with credibility. Subject matter expertise is a lot more critical in this relationship than with a mentor. One big difference is coaches are paid, so this relationship is more results-driven. More is at stake.

Earlier on, I mentioned my friend Cindy. She knows she wants to open a restaurant but she does not know how to get there. She's looking for a coach. Someone who specializes in this area, such as Donald Burns, The Restaurant Coach™.

As a coaching client, your goals should be to:

- Improve a professional skill set
- Tackle a short-term goal
- To find advice from an expert consultant

At different times in your career, both mentors and coaches will be able to play important roles in helping you succeed—as long as you are prepared to loosen your tight grip on the reins and let them help you move forward in the best way.

> *Allow influential, successful people into your life.*

TWO:
What are two areas in your life where you need to loosen control and bring in help?

_____
_____
_____
_____
_____
_____
_____
_____
_____
_____

THREE:
Consider these three criteria of needs to determine if you need a mentor or a coach:

A. Short-term help	B. Long-term help
A. General assistance	B. Specific assistance
A. Professional development	B. Strengthen a specific skill set

If you selected mostly A's, you need a mentor

If you selected mostly B's, you need a coach

ME:
How will it benefit you to have either the mentor or coach that you need? How can they lead you to being more, doing more, having more or all of the above?

_____
_____
_____
_____
_____
_____
_____
_____
_____
_____
_____
_____

| Perfectionism |

> "Go Boldly into The Unknown"

KIMBERLYBUCHANAN.COM

17
PERFECTIONISM

> *Examine what fears drive your perfectionism and look at how they are holding you back.*

Double-checking, second-guessing, hesitating, asking someone else's opinion, all of these habits are signs that you might be a perfectionist. You want to hold off sending the email or submitting the proposal until you are sure it's perfect, right?

When I first started out, I wanted everything to be perfect, too. I'm not sure that it was a confidence-problem, but it certainly held me back. I am sure that the quest for perfection is one of the biggest hurdles that we face as women as we set out on our journey to BE more. We are scared to make mistakes, and that fear can prevent us from taking the risks necessary to grow.

I've got news for you today. Guess what? You don't need to be perfect. You just need to start. And I promise you, once you get started you'll challenge yourself even more. You'll learn to take risks, try new things, and to continually get better. You'll be more concerned with the difference you are making than with whether your work is perfect.

In the beginning, my perfectionism stemmed from these three fears:

1. Making a mistake
2. Failing
3. The unknown

Yes, you read it right. Number three is the Fear of the Unknown. I often experienced anxiety over things I could not identify. I had no clue what I was afraid of, but that fear would hold me back from trying to grow. That's because I was simply afraid of the possible outcomes, even including the outcome that I would be successful.

You are likely standing still out of fear of that same unknown monster I just described, and it's time to let go of the unknown. Look the faceless monster straight in the eye and give yourself permission to try. Stop focusing on trying to do something perfectly and just do something.

If you make a mistake, you'll learn from it. If you fail, you'll learn what to do better in the future. If you encounter something new, and it's not as you thought it would be, you'll learn from it. As Ralph Nader once said, "Your best teacher is your last mistake." By re-framing failure and mistakes as opportunities to learn, you find the wisdom to avoid perfectionism.

You may not have it all together today. But examine what fears drive your perfectionism and look at how they are holding you back. With that knowledge, put yourself out there despite those fears and see what happens. If something goes wrong, you can either fix it or learn from it. But you'll never know until you try. You don't know if your risk is going to pay off or not, but it could pay off big time, so go boldly into the unknown.

Perfectionism can be debilitating and stifle you instead of making you strong. So, the next time you find yourself second-guessing yourself and feeding one of these fears, recognize what's happening so you can change course. Tell those fears they don't get to stop you and keep trying.

> *Re-frame failure and mistakes as opportunities to learn.*

TWO:
What are the two fears that drive you to be a perfectionist?

_____
_____
_____
_____
_____
_____
_____
_____
_____
_____

THREE:
What three things would you do if you weren't afraid you wouldn't do them perfectly? What action can you take to get started on them?

_____
_____
_____
_____
_____
_____
_____
_____
_____
_____

ME:
What will it feel like after you let go of the fears that make you a perfectionist? How can that help you Do, Be, and Have More?

_____
_____
_____
_____
_____
_____
_____
_____
_____
_____

| Trying To Do It All |

> "Successes multiply. One Victory will lead to two."

KIMBERLYBUCHANAN.COM

18
TRYING TO DO IT ALL

> *Focus on making your life better in one or two ways, instead of looking at everything that needs to be "fixed."*

About a year ago, I spent a week in Chicago on business. My hotel was across the street from Water Tower Place. In case you are not familiar, Water Tower Place is a Chicago landmark on the Magnificent Mile and renowned for its vast selection of over 100 stores. Beyond shopping, the eight-story mall also houses a number of restaurants and entertainment options. Trust me, ladies, Water Tower is our kind of place. Who can compete with the best shopping and the best food, all in one place?

On my last day of meetings, I was exhausted. But still, I decided to go to the mall and pick up a few items to bring home. Upon arriving, the first thing I looked for was the YOU ARE HERE kiosk or a map. Right away, I was reminded of how large Water Tower Place really is. As I browsed the listing of stores, I thought to myself, "I can't possibly get through this entire mall today. I need to look closely and decide which areas I really want to visit."

Sometimes, life, in general, is just like this. Although you may have many areas that are important to you and want to focus on making them all better, it's impossible to give 100 percent of your time to do and be everything. Trying to do it all can lead to overwhelm, stress, burnout, and MISTAKES.

You may recall when Oprah Winfrey sat down with the team on the CBS Morning Show. It was early April in 2012. The world was buzzing about the struggles of her newly launched OWN cable network. Oprah said to the CBS hosts, which included Charlie Rose and her best friend Gayle King, "If I knew then what I know now, I might have made some different choices. I would say if I were writing a book about it, I would call the book '101 mistakes.'" Oprah went on to mention that **one big mistake was launching the network while she still had her Chicago-based talk show.**

This is a fitting example of how someone was able to look back at the past mistake of trying to do it all at the same time, acknowledge everything that comes with those mistakes, and continue to move forward. Now that Oprah is no longer focusing on her talk show, OWN is strong and available in more than 80 million households and Miss. Oprah is still the queen of slayage, Black Girl Magic or whatever you prefer to label her "more."

I can't stress enough how important it is to focus on making your life better in one or two ways, instead of looking at everything that needs to be "fixed" and trying to tackle it all at the same time.

One victory will lead to two, two victories will lead to three, and so on. Give up a need to have it all. Instead, be victorious, one step at a time. When you really apply yourself to what you need to tackle first, you will have some early wins to build a foundation to work on bigger things as you move along.

There are no special medals for people who accomplish a lot of things all at the same time. One reason for that is probably that it's almost impossible to do so, and it's time to give up that illusion. If even Oprah can't do too many things at once, then it's perfectly fine that you can't, either. Don't try to do it all, but choose what you will do carefully, and do those things very well.

> *One victory will lead to two, two victories will lead to three, and so on.*

TWO:
What are the two most important things you should work on first?

_____
_____
_____
_____
_____
_____
_____
_____
_____
_____

THREE:
What three things are you going to let go of so you can do what's most important now?

_____
_____
_____
_____
_____
_____
_____
_____
_____
_____

ME:
What will change when you accomplish your first two areas of improvement? How will that progress lead you to being more, doing more, having more or all of the above?

_____
_____
_____
_____
_____
_____
_____
_____
_____

| A Need to Lead and Not Follow |

> "Be a Follower as well as a Leader."

19
A NEED TO LEAD AND NOT FOLLOW

> *Being a good follower makes you an even better leader.*

The more you learn, the more you grow. You should consider yourself a life-long learner. Not in the sense of sitting down in the classroom to learn, but in many different forms of learning. Sometimes it's tempting to think you know everything and can quit learning, especially if you are an expert in your field, but that's a dangerous feeling that can lead to stagnation. The way out of it is to be a follower as well as a leader.

I've dedicated my life to self-improvement and continuous learning in every way possible. Whether it be in the classroom, online, through travel experiences, or by meeting new people. I'm always willing to learn something new, which means I'm willing to follow other leaders and recognize that they have something to offer me.

Every time you set a new goal for yourself, evaluate where you are now as it relates to that goal and determine where you want to be in three, six, and twelve months. Because it is a goal, there is a need to close the gap between where you are and where you want to be. Most often, closing the gap requires you to be open to learning something new or developing in areas where you are lacking.

There's almost always someone who can help you in this development. However, you must be willing to accept that you cannot lead in this area. To learn and grow, you need to step back and be a follower. In this way, you'll discover that even though you may be an expert in your field, you are a novice in other fields.

For instance, if Cindy starts her restaurant and realizes she needs to advertise on social media, she will need to find experts to follow and learn from. She may also need to delegate this task to someone on her team who is more social media-savvy than she is. She doesn't have to be the master of every detail of her business, but she does have to find good leaders to follow therein.

You may be a boss or a supervisor, and you are a leader. But regardless of your position, you sometimes need to open yourself up to learning from others if you want to be a great supervisor or boss. Being a good follower makes you an even better leader. You could have team members you can give leadership positions to and follow in areas of which they may have insights to share with you.

It's perfectly okay to ask for help, too. When was the last time you approached someone on your team and said, "I have something I'd really like your help with. Can we discuss it now? If not, when?" Or, "My problem involves my perception of... and I know you have experience in this area. Is it ok for you and I to discuss this?"

Ronald E. Riggio, Ph.D., associate dean of the faculty at the Kravis Leadership Institute at Claremont McKenna College in Claremont, California, said, "Many of the same qualities that we admire in leaders—competence, motivation, intelligence—are the same qualities that we want in the very best followers. Moreover, leaders, regardless of their level, also need to follow." When you follow good leaders, you also learn new skills to bring back to your own leadership style.

Be open to change. Just because something has always been done your way, does not mean it's the best way. When you show yourself to be open to other's ideas and following their lead, you make them more likely to follow you and feel like a valuable member of your team. Letting go of your need to always be right and always take the front of the helm will empower the people around you and inspire them, so when it's right, follow other leaders.

> *When you follow good leaders, you also learn new skills to bring back to your own leadership.*

TWO:
What are the two areas in your life where you need to find someone to follow?

_____
_____
_____
_____
_____
_____
_____
_____
_____
_____

THREE:
What three people that are already in your life should you be letting lead more often?

_____
_____
_____
_____
_____
_____
_____
_____
_____
_____

ME:
How is being a follower more often going to help you be a better leader? How will changing this position help you **Do. Be.** and **Have More**?

_____
_____
_____
_____
_____
_____
_____
_____
_____
_____

| Competing |

> "There is Room for everyone's Excellence."

20 COMPETING

> *You see the glory, but don't know the story.*

See that other woman over there? She is not your competition. Neither is the one on social media or the one interviewed in your industry on that television show. You don't need to measure up to anyone else, and their success has nothing to do with your own.

Once you start to compare yourself to other people, doubts probably start running rampant in your head, and self-doubt can take hold and choke your growth. But guess, what? You don't ever have to feel this way. It is within your power to avoid the bad feelings from measuring yourself against others altogether.

Now, let's understand what I do and don't mean. It's okay to have an opinion about others whom you admire as role models. It's also okay to celebrate someone else's accomplishments. But that person is not you, and you shouldn't compare your own accomplishments against theirs. Have you ever heard someone say, "You see the glory, but you don't know the story?" Please keep that in your mind when you start to compare yourself to other people. You may not know what struggles they have overcome or that there are other things they haven't done that you have.

To compare yourself and using someone's accomplishments as a benchmark are two totally different things. It's ok to look at someone else as you set your goals. I often study people who I feel are successful or have reached some of the goals I desire to reach in my life. But never should you become resentful or jealous towards them because of it.

Pay close attention to your feelings and understand where they are coming from. Are they coming from a good or a bad place? If from a bad place, sit down with yourself and analyze why you feel this way. Then, try to turn that into something more productive or positive.

To stop comparing yourself to other people, work on these three areas:

1. *Accept yourself for exactly who you are*
2. *Appreciate the good qualities you have*
3. *Be thankful for how far you've already come*

When you accept yourself for who you are, then there's no accomplishment that anyone else can achieve that will diminish your own accomplishments from your viewpoint. You will find a place inside yourself to be happy for others without judging yourself in comparison. By letting yourself be who you are and accepting that, you feel freer to let others be who they are.

If you appreciate your good qualities, you won't be intimidated by the good qualities others possess. If someone is the best person at something in your field, you'll be happy for them because you know what you are best at, too. There is room for everyone's excellence.

Lastly, keeping an attitude of thankfulness will protect you from caring about anyone else's journey in comparison to your own. Celebrate all of your victories and run your own race. You can be so full of gratitude for your success that the idea of comparing your progress to anyone else's will seem ridiculous. It is! So, stop competing with others and focus on being your best self.

> *"Keeping an attitude of thankfulness will protect you from caring about anyone else's journey in comparison to your own."*

| Competing |

TWO:
What are two things you are thankful for overcoming?

_____
_____
_____
_____
_____
_____
_____
_____
_____
_____

THREE:
What three people are you competing with, and what can you change about how you see yourself to break that cycle?

_____
_____
_____
_____
_____
_____
_____
_____
_____
_____

ME:
How will your life improve when you quit competing with others? How is it going to benefit you to **Be, Do,** and **Have More** when you're finished taking action?

_____
_____
_____
_____
_____
_____
_____
_____
_____
_____

| Excuses |

> "Stop making excuses and start where you are today."

KIMBERLYBUCHANAN.COM

21
EXCUSES

> *Tell your excuses to pack their bags so you can get on your way to being more, having more, and doing the most.*

Are you making any of these excuses?

- *I could be doing a lot more, but I'm so scared to make a change.*
- *I know my business has room for growth, but I don't' have any more time to work on it.*
- *I gave up when I had kids, and they have to come first.*
- *I'm spending so much time at work, and everything else is falling apart.*
- *I'm making money, but I could be making more, and I am afraid to try in case I fail.*
- *I'm not happy, but I'm scared I'll fail if I try something new.*
- *I like what I do, but I need to walk away. It's too much to balance.*
- *I'm stuck.*
- *I've been doing this for so long, I don't know how to start trying something new.*

I could go on and on with this list. It was developed by 100 women I surveyed from several countries back in 2016. These women were under stress, felt like they were pulled in a million different directions, doubted themselves, and many were on the verge of total burnout.

I get it. My biggest excuse was telling myself, "I'll start Monday." That was my excuse for everything. It was even my excuse for starting this book. I can't tell you how many Monday's I promised myself I would start writing this book. Monday after Monday after Monday would come and go. Once I stopped the excuses and just did it, I wrote this book in less than two weeks from start to finish.

Are you sabotaging your dreams on your road to a better you by blaming everyone and everything around you? Are you blaming it on a difficult childhood? A bad relationship? A terrible boss? Unless you accept 100% responsibility for everything from your finances, to your health, to your future, nothing in life will ever change. It's time for it to stop now and you are the only person that can stop it.

Stop making excuses and start where you are today. The next time you think about your dream and then follow with an excuse, write it down. If it looks anything like the list I just outlined, you can overcome it. That's because excuses are smoke screens. In contrast, obstacles are real problems to solve. The difference is that an excuse is an argument within yourself that is fear-based, and you only need yourself to overcome them. With the tools you have right now, tell your excuses to pack their bags so you can get on your way to being more, having more, and doing the most for the life you desire to live.

It might not be easy at first, and some excuses will be harder to dispel than others, but the more you recognize your excuses and don't give them power, the better you will be at not giving into them.

If you're ready to take control of your success, business, time, finances, etc., stick with me. Read the last few pages of this book. I think you'll be pleasantly surprised by how easy it is to continue your journey.

> *The more you recognize your excuses and don't give them power, the better you will be at not giving into them.*

TWO:

What are two excuses you've been telling yourself for far too long? Write them down.?

_____
_____
_____
_____
_____
_____
_____
_____
_____
_____

THREE:

What three actions do you plan to take to move forward and stop making excuses?

_____
_____
_____
_____
_____
_____
_____
_____
_____
_____

ME:

How can you benefit when you no longer give in to your excuses? How will this lead you to being more, doing more, having more or all of the above?

_____
_____
_____
_____
_____
_____
_____
_____

| Unlock Your Potential |

"Let's Continue Your

| Continuing Your Journey |

Journey, Together..;,

KIMBERLYBUCHANAN.COM | 137 |

| Continuing Your Journey |

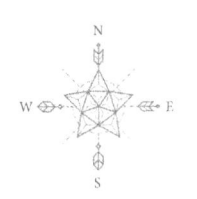

> *Start right where you are, with only what you have. Nothing more is required.*

Now that you've shed the 21 Things that were holding you back from being, doing, and having more, how do you feel? Are you lighter, more clear-headed? I know how amazing it feels after completing the exercises in each chapter of this book and having the majority of your biggest hurdles, and all the excuses, behind you.

Now I need to let you in on a little secret.

There's still work ahead. You know it in your heart already. After changing this much, you know you are capable of more. And sure, you will have those days when you don't feel like doing anything more, but that's okay. You know why? Because you're not alone. I welcome you to my support system of women who are ready to pick you up when you are low, and you can all work together to keep reaching for your potential.

You are **FREE** to unlock the next chapter of your journey. Don't breeze through the last few pages of this book and place it on the shelf among others. This book is more than that. It's a gateway to an entire new you and a full support system. Take advantage of the resources on the following pages, and a community full of women who will be beside you on this journey.

Cheers to you, my friend.
Be More. Do More. Have More.

– Kimberly

> *I've assembled that Dream Team for you, already.*

The Growth Network

In Chapter 9 of this book, we discussed a need to surround yourself with people who will Lift you up and Thrust you toward your potential. I want you to succeed in this area, so I assembled that Dream Team for you, already. If you are looking to get plugged into a network of positive women who are working on being more, doing more and having more every day, we have a resource for you.

Through The Growth Network you can gain:

- Support on your journey
- Resources from Kimberly
- Feedback from others in the group
- Exclusive offers and previews

**To join The Growth Network, visit:
unlockyourpotentialbook.com**

Growth Coaching

Do you require more individualized attention? Do you have specific goals you are trying to reach within the next 3 to 18 months and are not sure how to get there? I am ready to coach you through the process one-on-one; as we continue to **Unlock Your Potential.**

To schedule your first 30-minute session for FREE.

Visit: www.kimberlybuchanan.com/connect

Tell Us About It

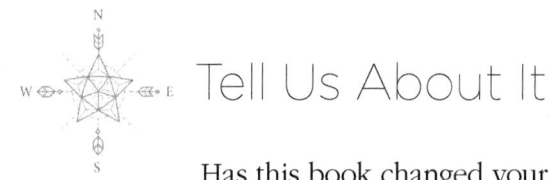

Has this book changed your life for the better? We want to hear the story about how this book has helped you unlock your potential. Please share your biggest takeaways and ask for any help you need by emailing us at info@kimberlybuchanan.com